W9-BVU-610

THE Magic OF Mozart

MOZART, *THE MAGIC FLUTE,* AND THE SALZBURG MARIONETTES

BY *Ellen Switzer*   PHOTOGRAPHS BY *Costas*

A JEAN KARL BOOK

ATHENEUM BOOKS FOR YOUNG READERS

Atheneum Books for Young Readers
An imprint of Simon & Schuster Children's Publishing Division
1230 Avenue of the Americas
New York, NY 10020

Text copyright © 1995 by Ellen Switzer
Photographs copyright © 1995 by Costas
All rights reserved including the right of
reproduction in whole or in part in any form.

First edition
Printed in the United States of America
10   9   8   7   6   5   4   3   2   1
The text of this book is set in 12-point Goudy Old Style and Avant Garde Book.
Book design by Kimberly M. Adlerman

Library of Congress Cataloging-in-Publication Data
Switzer, Ellen Eichenwald.
The magic of Mozart: The magic flute, and the Salzburg marionettes / by Ellen Switzer;
photographs by Costas. — 1st ed.
p.   cm.
"A Jean Karl book."
Includes bibliographical references.
ISBN 0-689-31851-0
1. Mozart, Wolfgang Amadeus, 1756–1791.   2. Mozart, Wolfgang
Amadeus, 1756–1791.   Zauberflöte.   3. Salzburger Marionettentheater. [1. Mozart,
Wolfgang Amadeus, 1756–1791.   2. Composers.]   I. Costas, ill.
ML410.M9S93   1995
782.1—dc20   93-47890
Summary: A retelling of Mozart's The Magic Flute, including a biographical
section about Mozart and a behind-the-scenes account of a performance
of the work by the Salzburger Marionettentheater, illustrated with photographs.

To Corey, Rebecca, and Jesse

We wish to express our profound gratitude to Frau Gretl Aicher, who spent hours of her valuable time with us explaining the history of the puppets, how they are created and worked, and even opened the theater to provide special lighting for the few scenes that were difficult to photograph with regular performance lights. We also wish to thank her staff, who were kind and helpful to us at all times, and from whom we learned a great deal.

Our thanks also to Günther Schneider-Siemssen, who allowed us to photograph and use in this book his remarkable scenery for this production of *The Magic Flute*.

ES
Costas

KENT STATE UNIVERSITY LIBRARY, KENT, OHIO

Contents

INTRODUCTION 1

PART I : *Mozart* 5
   1. Mozart the Wunderkind 7
   2. Traveling 12
   3. The Years When Nothing Worked—Except the Music 17
   4. First Love 20
   5. Constanze and First Opera 24
   6. Marriage and Family 28
   7. Marriage in Real Life and in Opera 30
   8. Last Years 35

PART II : The Magic Flute: *The Story* 43

PART III : *The Salzburg Marionettes* 73
   1. Kinds of Puppets 75
   2. The Salzburg Marionettes: Actors on Strings 80
   3. Gretl Aicher: The Present and the Future 87

BIBLIOGRAPHY 90

Introduction

The first glimmer of an idea for a book often comes to me from something that happened when I was a young child. That is true of *The Magic of Mozart*.

I remember once, late at night, waking up and hearing music being played on the phonograph downstairs. I could faintly hear the voice of a woman singing music I had never heard before. That voice could do amazing things—it could soar to high notes that seemed impossible for any human being to produce. The notes followed each other at amazing speed.

Later I would learn that women with voices like that are called coloratura sopranos (those who use elaborate embellishments in their singing) and that there are quite a number of such singers in the world. But at the time the voice sounded a bit like a bird, and a bit like the ghost of a Swiss yodeler. I asked to hear the record the next day, and someone played it for me. It was Mozart's *The Magic Flute*, and the lady with the amazing voice was a character called the Queen of the Night.

I loved the whole opera, which luckily was in German, my native language, and the only language I knew at that time. Then someone read me the story. It seemed fascinating with its mysterious magicians, a beautiful, evil lady, and, of course, a handsome prince in love with a princess. Most interesting was a couple called Papageno and Papagena, two beings who were half bird, half human.

A few years later I was taken to see the opera, which on stage turned out to be much less magical than it was in my imagination. I had pictured the Queen of the Night as a gorgeously glamorous, though somewhat frightening, character who could move as well as sing at an amazing speed. Instead, on the stage, I saw a rather solid-looking blonde who reminded me of my math teacher. The music was fine, but the woman certainly was not the Queen of the Night as I had thought of her.

Papageno, whom I had always imagined as the kind of character who could hop, run, and even fly, turned out to be an overweight little man who spent most of his time just standing around while singing all that wonderful music. Papagena looked more like a fat hen than a delicate little nightingale.

In the years after, I saw many versions of *The Magic Flute* done by several opera companies. I always loved the music, but the performance never fit what I had imagined when I was a little girl. Then one Christmas season, a marionette company from Salzburg, Austria, came to New York's Lincoln Center. I had heard of them. They specialized in Mozart operas, and my friends told me they were wonderful. My friends were right. For the first time I saw the Queen of the Night exactly as I had always imagined her, gorgeous and evil. Papageno and Papagena could not only sing but fly like beautiful birds. Even the two main characters, who have always seemed a little boring to me, Prince Tamino and Princess Pamina, were so beautiful and charming that one could believe the rather unlikely story that they had fallen madly in love without even meeting.

No human being could really play these characters the way I had imagined them. But this group of marionettes was exactly right. They moved like human beings, yet they also somehow had the magic of characters in a fairy tale. So I decided to write the story of *The Magic Flute* and illustrate it with photographs of the Salzburg Marionettes, taken by my favorite photographer, and good friend, Costas. He, like I, understood the special magic of this opera and those puppets who were at once so human and so otherworldly. So, here is the result of our joint efforts. The text begins with something about Mozart, because without him *The Magic Flute* would not exist. Then there is the story the opera tells. And finally there is something about the puppets and those who operate them. I hope the book does justice to the opera, to those wonderful marionettes, and most of all to Mozart, who may have been the greatest artist of all time.

P · A · R · T · I

Mozart

Mozart the Wunderkind

Salzburg, Austria, is a lovely town, divided by a river that runs between two hilly sections. On one side, overlooking the town, is a medieval castle, and on the other side of the river are many beautiful old churches and houses and shops, all arranged along narrow old streets.

In the summer Salzburg can be hot and humid, with gray skies and heavy showers; and in the winter it can be freezing cold and damp with sleet and snow.

It was on just such a winter night that a tiny, scrawny infant was born to Leopold and Anna Maria Mozart, a middle-class couple, who lived on the side of town without the castle.

The entire house had one fireplace. The neighborhood women who attended the birth wore gloves and heavy clothing in the bedroom where the baby was born. They probably could see their breath in the cold, damp air. Most of these women did not expect the infant to live. In those days the life of an infant was fragile, even if a baby was bigger and healthier than the one they now tried to keep as warm as possible in his mother's bed.

Today, such an undersized infant would be transferred to a previously warmed incubator to maintain his body heat. Lots of blankets and a cradle near the fireplace would have been the correct medical treatment then. However, since the baby seemed so close to death, everybody worried more about his soul than his body. Dying unbaptized would have been the worst disaster. So the infant was taken to the Salzburg Cathedral to be baptized almost as soon as he was born.

Someone who was present at the ceremony wrote later that pieces of ice were floating on the water in the baptismal font.

The feeble little boy was given the very long name, Johannes Chrysostomus Wolfgangus Theophilus Mozart. Theophilus is a Greek name that means "love of God." Later Leopold, after a trip to Italy, translated this into the more elegant sounding Italian version, Amadeus. He also added another lengthy name to the list, Sigismundus, after the local archbishop whom he thought to flatter into giving him a better position. Leopold was a minor composer and assistant conductor at the archbishop's court, a position that gave him respectability, but not enough money to provide a good life for his family. The archbishop, unfortunately, did not pay the slightest attention to the compliment, and Leopold Mozart received neither the promotion nor the raise for which he had hoped.

Even though the baby's birth did not improve the family's finances, he surprised everybody by not dying. Not only did he survive his difficult birth and that cold trip to the cathedral, he actually thrived. And, as soon as he was old enough to make decisions about such matters as names, he chose to keep only two of them: Wolfgang Amadeus. To friends and relatives he was known as Wolferl, or sometimes Wolfie.

Out of the seven children Mozart's mother bore, only two survived: a girl, Marianne (known all her life as Nannerl), and the youngest, Wolferl. Nannerl was almost five years older than her brother. The children grew up quite happily.

Nannerl looked healthy and pretty, with her blue eyes and light blond hair. Wolferl grew into a toddler who was considered particularly even-tempered and loving. The family had moved into a more luxurious home, a house that is now the Mozart Museum, with enough room so that the parlor could be used for entertaining. In that house, most of the guests were musicians, and often during an evening or a late afternoon, the parents and their guests entertained each other with private concerts.

Everything went smoothly as long as the mother and two children left all decisions to the father, who ruled the household like a king and allowed no contradictions to whatever decisions he made.

Noticing that his daughter showed some talent at the clavier (an early version of today's piano), Leopold decided to give her lessons. She would serve as a kind of advertisement for his teaching ability, helping him to get more and richer pupils.

When he was working with the little girl, he hardly noticed that Wolferl, his three year old, would drop whatever he was doing and sit on the floor, watching the lessons with breathless attention. Sometimes he would try to play a chord after Nannerl had finished, even when his hands were still too small to reach the keys. When he was only four, he started begging his father for lessons, and Leopold, sensing that this child might have a particular talent, agreed.

After about a year, Wolferl could play better than his sister. He clearly loved music, even more than his pet canary, who, before Mozart found the clavier, had been his favorite companion. He sat for hours a day at the instrument, learning harder and harder pieces, often playing perfectly something he had heard only once or twice. His father was soon convinced that the little boy was a genuine "wunderkind" (a young genius), who would make his mark on the world. Now Wolferl was often the featured player at home concerts, admired not only by his parents, but by all the guest musicians.

Not only did Wolfie play, but he began to compose. When he was just four years old, he was found one day at his father's music desk, with ink all over his face and hands, writing what looked like notes on music paper. Instead of scolding him for making such a mess, his father asked to see what he was doing. Wolferl informed him that he was writing a concerto. His father and two guest musicians, who happened to have dropped in for their afternoon coffee with whipped cream, looked at the paper and saw that Wolferl had actually written what could be interpreted as a melody.

Wolfie continued to try to write music, which got less ink spotted and more melodic by the month. Not only was he able to play the clavier and write delightful tunes by age five, he also seemed able to play instruments for which he had never had lessons. For instance, when a court violinist came to the house with another friend to play trios with Leopold, Wolferl tried to join in with the tiny children's violin that had been given to him as a present. He made mistakes, but not enough to ruin the rehearsal. It was obvious he would be able to learn this instrument as quickly as he had the clavier, and Leopold added violin lessons to those he gave at the keyboard.

A year later Wolferl picked up a trumpet left in the music room by a guest and flawlessly played one of his favorite tunes.

When Wolferl was six, Leopold decided that the time had come to use his children to improve the family's fame and fortune, even if that meant leaving Salzburg and taking the youngsters to some of the larger, more sophisticated, richer cities of Austria and other European countries. There the children might be invited to give concerts at the homes of wealthy and noble people, and be richly rewarded for their efforts.

Even today, taking two young children on the long and exhausting journey Leopold planned might present some difficulties. But in Mozart's day there were no airplanes, or even trains or buses. There were only horses and coaches. The coaches Leopold could afford to hire were likely to be slow, freezing in the winter, broiling hot in the summer, often dirty, and generally unsafe.

To add to the difficulty of travel, the inns and posthouses that dotted the European landscape were generally dirty and miserable. The kind of public inns Leopold could afford were likely to be cold in the winter, with heat only in the public rooms, not the rooms where the guests slept. Bedding was rarely changed. Sheets were not washed from one set of guests to another. Of course, there was no running water and no other kind of plumbing. Many of these inns did not even have outhouses. There were lice, rats, and other vermin.

Leopold Mozart was putting his children in real danger by taking them on the long trip he had planned, and chances are he knew it. But he was determined to go and to take both children.

Nannerl played the clavier very well, although not nearly as expertly as her brother. The father thought, however, that two talented children would receive more attention than just one, even if the one was a genuine wunderkind. The children's mother was not invited to go along. She did not play an instrument and, therefore, could add nothing to either the performances or the publicity that Leopold planned for Wolferl and Nannerl.

C·H·A·P·T·E·R · 2

Traveling

It was September 1761, just as the cold rains started to descend on Austria and Germany, when Mozart's public career began. He was to spend most of his youth on the road. As a child star he was often wildly successful at the castles and courts the family visited. Like many attractive, very young performers, he was admired as much for his youthful charm as his musical ability, a fact that apparently escaped Leopold's notice. He thought of the journey as only the beginning of a brilliant future.

The children were much admired in several small German towns, but the concerts brought in little money. Leopold thought that this would change when they hit Vienna and played for the royal court. And at first it seemed as if he were right.

The family's stay in Vienna was a triumph. Mozart never forgot the wonderful days he spent there, and from that time on always preferred Vienna to Salzburg. The empress, who had borne sixteen children herself, took to the Mozart youngsters immediately. Apparently Wolferl took to her as well. Reports indicate that the first time he met her he made the polite bow that was expected and then jumped on her lap and kissed her.

The little princes and princesses also loved their new court musicians, whom they treated as friends. They gave them toys, fed them candy, and played duets with them on the clavier. But when the Mozart children fell ill, they were soon forgotten; when they recovered, Leopold decided to take them to Paris.

The Mozart family arrived in Paris in the middle of November 1763. Now, Paris is considered one of the most beautiful cities in the world, but in those days it seemed to most non-Parisians to be an exceptionally dirty, disorganized place.

The French court astounded the Mozarts, who had expected to find the kind of clean, well-organized family life they had seen at the Austrian imperial court. The French palaces looked splendid on the outside, but on the inside were almost as dirty as the streets. Also, they were icy cold in the winter.

However, the children charmed the court in Paris as they had in Austria, and the pay was good. So Leopold insisted on staying. The one problem was that they were treated like servants. For instance, they were invited to the state dinner on New Year's Day 1764, but the invitation did not include food. They were asked to stand behind the royal chairs and watch the king and the nobles eat a large meal. Both children were hungry (apparently they had expected to be fed), but nothing was offered. Wolferl was a little luckier than the rest of the Mozarts. He was placed behind the queen's chair, and she must have seen that his eyes followed every bite she took. At any rate, she fed him bits of food from the table. Perhaps it was an experience like this that prompted the adult Mozart to decide that he would not put himself in a situation where musicians were treated worse than servants, and to make the servants in his operas wise and attractive.

Then on June 6, 1765, disaster struck. Wolfgang became seriously ill. In fact, he almost died. Leopold did not realize how close he had come to losing his son. This illness would affect his health for the rest of his life. He would never again be completely healthy, even after his apparent recovery. As soon as Wolfgang was well enough to sit at the clavier again, Leopold accepted invitations for his two children to play concerts in Hungary, which meant another long carriage ride through rugged country. When they arrived, Wolfgang was not really well enough to play, so the concerts were not a success. There was nothing to do but return to Salzburg.

Back in Salzburg Leopold immediately began planning the next long trip. They would return to Paris. This time, after the experience with Wolfgang's illness, Mama Mozart was asked to come on the journey, which was meant to last six months, but eventually took three years.

After considerable success in Paris, the family crossed the channel to England, where the public, like most others, was entranced by the two children who looked so charming and played like talented adults. In London, Mozart, now age eight, wrote his first symphonies and many piano and violin pieces. The event he remembered most vividly all his life was his first visit to the opera. Later he said that this first impression convinced him that he would like to become a great opera composer. The family also met many of the great and famous musicians of their time, who were welcome at the London court and who assured Leopold that his young son was indeed a very special talent.

Only a letter from the Salzburg diocese warning Leopold that he would be fired if he did not return to his job persuaded the parents that they must go home, a prospect that did not appeal to them at all. But after another lengthy journey with more concerts on the way, they did return.

When Leopold went to report to the archbishop, he found out that he still had his job. But he also learned that his salary, which he thought had been safely put away for him during his absence, had stopped long before. He was informed that from now on he would be paid only when he was actually in Salzburg working at his assigned tasks.

The children gave concerts in their hometown, earning what they could to supplement the family's meager income. The lessons with their father continued. Leopold also managed to get several local composers, one of whom had been a student of Johann Sebastian Bach, to give lessons in composition to his son. For two years, Wolfgang got the kind of education he needed to do the extraordinary work he produced in his later years.

For two years Mozart was actually able to stay in one place and live a relatively normal life. Before he reached his teen years, he was given a minor post by the archbishop, which unfortunately paid nothing, but which gave him an opportunity to compose music on commission, usually for some special occasion in the cathedral. The music he was called upon to compose had to include singers, soloists or choirs, or both, along with an organ. He had had little training in this type of music, but, as always, he learned fast. The experience was enormously helpful to him later, when he seriously began to compose operas.

Leopold approved of his young son's desire to write operas. Operas were, in those days, the way to fame and fortune. In fact, Leopold decided that Wolfgang should learn more about operatic performances in Italy, especially Milan, where the most famous opera house in the world was located. So off to Milan they went.

Mozart loved Milan. He went to the opera every night that he did not have to perform himself. There were also opera houses in two smaller cities through which they traveled, Mantua and Parma. In both, the boy spent hours at rehearsals, listening to composers exchange information, watching the conductor, and making friends with the singers. He learned as much about opera in a few months as he had in all his previous training.

At Christmastime a nobleman in Milan, who had befriended the Mozarts, actually commissioned an opera, and it was performed at the Milan Opera House once. Compared with the masterpieces Mozart would later produce, it sounded like the work of a very young, inexperienced composer, but it gave Wolfgang the kind of practice he needed to develop his operatic skills.

After another short trip to Milan, the Mozarts traveled back to Salzburg, where they remained for the next six years. During that time Mozart grew from an attractive and lovable little boy into a rather homely adolescent, with a short and spindly body, a long nose, and a short chin. One of the reasons for his early success had been that he was a child. Like so many child stars through the centuries, when he stopped being cute and adorable, he got little work. Yet Mozart, hidden from public view, was growing from an appealing and talented little boy into one of the greatest musical geniuses the world has ever known.

The Years When Nothing Worked—Except the Music

The six years Mozart spent in Salzburg with his family served only to make him realize that he detested his hometown. He found it boring, restrictive, hypocritical, and snobbish.

The old archbishop had finally died, but the new one, Hieronymus, was even stingier and more coldly contemptuous of his court musicians than his predecessor. Leopold still was only the assistant Kapellmeister (conductor). Also, in spite of repeated requests, the archbishop refused to appoint Wolfgang to any respectable situation. He gave him 150 gulden a year (about $100) to compose whatever was asked of him, which included innumerable pieces of church music and almost monthly requests for serenades, concertos, and other nonreligious compositions to be played at parties and at court.

During those six years Mozart composed many of his best symphonies. He also wrote a great many pieces of chamber music, several concertos for a variety of instruments, marches, and dances for special occasions, all without any recognition of his talent or his hard work.

He made friends among the other court musicians, who recognized his special qualities, but were also in direct competition with him for the few commissions and sponsored concerts that were available.

During the time that Mozart lived in his father's house, the relationship between father and son became more and more strained. Leopold appreciated his son's genius. He firmly believed the wunderkind had turned into a musician of unusual ability. But much as he loved and approved of his son's music, he disapproved of his behavior. Why would young Mozart not make the most of his gifts? Why would he not visit the court regularly, try to make friends with the minor nobility, and so gain access to the even more important aristocrats at Salzburg? Why did he continually refuse to compromise and write the kind of popular music that seemed to be to the court's liking? Why were all of his best friends other court musicians, and why did he spend so much time with young men who were, in Leopold's opinion, socially below him, playing cards in taverns and coffeehouses?

He continued to treat his son like a child, which he no longer was. And Mozart, in spite of his love and respect for his father, became more and more resentful.

Mozart wanted to leave Salzburg to give concerts in other cities. Most of all, he wished to try for commissions to compose operas. He knew he needed a collaborator to write the story texts that, in his opinion, a good opera needed. Opera, he believed, needed to be good theater as well as an occasion for various characters to burst into song. He wanted to see real, believable people on the stage. He wanted to eliminate much of the artificiality in operas that were being written. And he knew that there was no opportunity to write this kind of opera in Salzburg. So he finally informed his father that he was leaving, with or without the permission of the archbishop, who was not eager to see his poorly paid composer leave town.

Leopold was appalled. If his son quit, he, too, might be fired. And then how would the family live? But young Mozart could be as firm as he was gentle. He went to see the archbishop, told him that he wanted an indefinite leave, and was promptly dismissed.

That meant Wolfgang could go, but he would be going out into the world alone, away from strict parental control. "Impossible," Leopold said. Mozart's mother would have to accompany her son. She was to report, preferably in daily letters, exactly what was happening, and how young Mozart was behaving and progressing.

Mozart, according to his letters, was delighted to have Mama instead of Papa along on this trip. She was helpful, gentle, good-humored, and, of course, considerably less bossy than his father. So, on September 3, 1777 (unfortunately just as the cold weather was starting), they took off. Mozart hoped that this would be the last he would see of Salzburg for a long time. His mother hoped that she would be able to go home as soon as possible. She never did.

First Love

Mother and son traveled to several German cities, including Mannheim. Mannheim had an excellent court orchestra for which an old friend of the family played the flute. Mozart had always disliked the flute, but when the opportunity arose he decided to accept a commission to compose two flute concertos. Both have wonderful melodies that make the instrument sound almost like a human voice, and they are as easy to listen to as they are difficult to play.

While he traveled, Mozart was composing profusely, and needed to have some of his music copied. In Mannheim, an excellent copier, Friedolin Weber, was recommended to him and soon became a friend. Copiers were at the lowest end of the music world's social scale. In today's world, they would rank somewhere between the file clerk and the mail-room worker in the hierarchy of an office. Even worse, from Mama Mozart's point of view, Weber was much poorer than the Mozarts, had a hard-drinking wife with a bad reputation, and had too many children, including three daughters who would need husbands and dowries. He and his family were definitely not fit companions for her son. This information was conveyed to Leopold, who replied to his son in one of his almost daily nagging letters.

Now young Mozart really rebelled against his father. Not only did he like the Weber family (with the exception of the mother), he was fascinated by one of the daughters, Aloysia, an exceedingly pretty teenager, who was already a featured singer at the local opera.

She was superbly gifted as a musician. Like young Mozart, she could repeat a melody perfectly after having heard it only once. Mozart, who loved composing for the female voice, thought he had found the perfect singer. She also had shiny black hair, a lovely complexion, huge dark eyes, and a finely developed figure. Within days Mozart was madly in love with her, and she seemed to return his affection. From then on he spent most of his time at the Webers', working with Aloysia on new songs, polishing her singing technique, and holding hands under the piano.

Both Mama and Papa Mozart were appalled, and finally because there seemed to be no way for Mozart to make money in Mannheim he had to leave. Leopold said he must go back to Paris.

Mozart hoped that though his stay in Mannheim was at an end, his romance would continue. He asked Aloysia to wait for him, and she agreed. Then, tearfully, he departed with his mother, not for Salzburg as she would have liked, but for Paris.

At home Leopold waited for letters announcing new and greater triumphs. He had supplied his son with at least fifty letters of introduction, most addressed to people of rank whom he himself knew only second- or thirdhand. He expected young Mozart to pay court to all of them and land the kind of position that befit his talents.

Mozart tried. He hated those visits. He had to bow, scrape, and humiliate himself, often before the potential patron's assistants or secretaries, who made no secret of their contempt for a young man who did not look like a Parisian dandy. Everything was going wrong. There was no work, no chance of success. He missed Aloysia desperately and wrote her often, but her letters became fewer and fewer, and finally stopped altogether. Worst of all, there was almost no money.

Even the usually cheerful Anna Maria was becoming depressed. She knew no one in Paris and spent day after day and night after night in a dark, airless attic room, all the housing they could afford. What's worse, she started to lose weight and began to complain of feeling ill. Mozart repeatedly wrote to his father begging him to let them come home, if not for his sake, then for his mother's.

Anna Maria's health deteriorated from week to week. Young Mozart was too inexperienced to realize that she was critically ill. He did know that she needed medical attention, but had little money to pay a doctor. Eventually, without needed help, she died.

Mozart had to borrow money to bury Anna Maria and was now penniless. He decided, on his own, without his father's permission, to leave Paris and go back to Salzburg. However, instead of going directly home, he stopped off in Munich where his beloved Aloysia had become a star performer at the opera. He was sure that, although he had not heard from her for months, she still loved him.

Aloysia was no longer living with her family, though they had moved to Munich with her. Instead, she had a large apartment of her own in the best section of the city. Her fame and beauty had attracted a swarm of admirers who paid most of her bills and showered her with expensive clothes and jewelry.

Mozart found her at a large party in her home and rushed up to her eagerly, grasping her hand and kissing it passionately. She looked at him as if she did not recognize him, pulled away her hand and continued flirting and laughing with all the richly dressed, elegant young men around her. When he turned to look, he realized that the whole group was laughing at him, the country bumpkin who had the nerve to kiss the hand of one of the most popular young women in town. He was not only bitterly hurt, he despised what he saw as snobbism and disloyalty. He sat down at the piano and sang a very vulgar song about women who allow themselves to be kept by those who will only use them and who forget their real friends. Then he left the room both heartbroken and furious.

For Mozart, an important part of his life was over. He had failed to gain the success his father had expected of him. He had no money. He had lost both his mother and the woman he loved. He also realized that he was no longer an adolescent and that he could not depend on others to direct his life. From now on he was on his own, a man who would have to live as best he could by his own skill, talent, and principles.

Some critics think that Aloysia may have been his model for the Queen of the Night in *The Magic Flute*. She had turned out to be hard-hearted, vain, and treacherous. What's more, she had the kind of voice that was needed for the part. At any rate, her rejection made him look at his future realistically for the first time.

Constanze and First Opera

Mozart remained in Munich only for a short time. When his father wrote to him that the archbishop had finally agreed to give Wolfgang a regular (and Leopold hinted "well-paid") position, he returned. This time the archbishop actually came through with a job as court organist. (Mozart had managed to teach himself to play the organ along with all the other musical instruments he had mastered.)

Although he still hated living in Salzburg, back under his father's watchful eyes and constant criticism, he took advantage of his new financial security. Also, his position was not demanding. He had plenty of time to compose symphonies, concertos, and other music. The trouble was, he was treated as badly as ever. He was expected to live and behave like any of the court's other servants. And he made up his mind that as soon as other musical possibilities presented themselves, he would leave again.

During this period, Mozart met a man who would become important to him in later life and take part in the writing of *The Magic Flute*. A traveling theatrical company arrived to do a few performances in Salzburg. The director,

Emanuel Schickaneder, was friendly and clever. Furthermore, he was some-one with whom Mozart could discuss his favorite subject, opera. Schick-aneder had never created an opera, but he had always wanted to attempt one. He discussed with Mozart the possibility that sometime in the future they might collaborate on a fairy tale to be sung in German, not Italian, so that it would be entertainment for the general public, not just the court. Many years later they worked together on just such an opera, *The Magic Flute*.

One day in Salzburg, Mozart encountered the whole Weber family. They were just passing through, but Wolfgang learned that Aloysia had re-ceived a very important appointment at the National Theater in Vienna. What's more, the Webers said, Emperor Joseph had decided that he would try to produce German operas, using German composers, singers, and other musicians. This idea delighted Mozart, but the presence of the Webers made Leopold worried and angry, especially when he noted that Wolfgang was becoming interested in Aloysia's younger sister, Constanze.

Although she was not as beautiful, or nearly as talented a musician as Aloysia, she had a fine figure, large eyes, a little turned up nose, and a lovely complexion. Most important of all, it was clear she thought Mozart was just about the most exciting young man she had ever met.

The Webers left Salzburg, and soon after, friends in Munich managed to obtain a commission for Mozart to write the music for a full-length opera, to be performed at the Royal Opera House in the winter of 1781. By now Mozart was mature enough to realize that the promise of one opera was not enough to make him pack up his bags and leave his job for an uncertain fu-ture in the big city. Since he had plenty of time to compose at home, when he got his contract, he began at once.

Unfortunately, the story of the opera that had been provided was both illogical and boring. By now Mozart was realistic enough to understand that new and unknown opera composers didn't have many choices. So he de-cided to bring the whole work to life with music.

The opera, called *Idomeneo*, was a strange version of an ancient Greek legend about the daughter of King Agamemnon of Greece, who insists on sacrificing her to the gods to change the course of the wind. He needs more favorable weather so that his ships, carrying the army, can take off for Troy to fight the Trojan wars. For some reason, the author of the opera text had changed the daughter into a son. To Mozart, well-versed in Greek mythology, this, along with many other details, did not make sense.

There were other causes for dissatisfaction: The work was written in Italian, not in German as Mozart had hoped, and the style of the music was to conform to French and Italian standards. But this was an important commission, and Mozart was determined to write an opera that was not a carbon copy of many of the classical works he had seen and heard.

The opera was given for the first time in January 1781 and was an instant success. The critics wrote that it was somehow different from other operas. There was more importance given to the orchestra than in most operas in the Italian style. The instruments set the atmosphere and they supported and blended with the voices of the singers. It was also noted that *Idomeneo* was livelier and more enjoyable than most operas given in Munich and Vienna and that "hardly anybody went to sleep during the performance."

Shortly after this success, Mozart received a letter from his employer, the archbishop of Salzburg, ordering him to go to Vienna at once. The archbishop had been asked to make a state visit to the city, and he was taking his court, including his musicians, with him. Obviously Mozart, with his new fame, was expected to be present.

Mozart arrived in Vienna in the early spring, when that city is at its loveliest. He was now twenty-five years old and had won a major success with his opera, so that he was known to potential patrons and certainly to many other musicians. He expected to make new connections, perhaps get another opera commission, and play many concerts at the musicals given regularly by the local aristocracy. But he had not reckoned with the archbishop. Mozart was informed that he would not be allowed to rent his own quarters. He must live in the suite of rooms his employer had taken for himself and his staff. Wolfgang's room was small and cramped, smaller in fact than that of the upper servants. Also, he was to eat with the servants. "Two valets sit at the head of the table, but I have at least the honor of sitting above the two cooks," he wrote his father in disgust. He also announced to his father that he was going to quit the archbishop's service altogether.

Leopold bombarded him with letters threatening and begging him to remain on the archbishop's staff, but Wolfgang did what he wanted to do—he resigned. He became his own master, getting commissions and concerts wherever he could find them. His financial future might be uncertain, but no one would ever be able to attack his dignity as a musician and as a human being again.

Marriage and Family

When Mozart left the archbishop's lodging, he had enough money to take a room at a reasonably good inn or even rent a small apartment. But he wanted a home. The closest place to a home that he could think of was the Webers' house, where Mrs. Weber had begun to take regular boarders. Living with the Webers was also helpful because he was becoming more and more interested in Constanze, who was now eighteen years old.

Mozart tried to get Leopold's approval to marry Constanze. He assured his father that she would be a perfect wife. But Leopold refused to sanction the marriage and instead urged Mozart to come back to Salzburg.

Almost immediately after he received a letter from his father demanding that he return to Salzburg, Mozart got his second major commission to write music for an opera. It was to be based on a libretto (the words sung in the opera) written by a German poet (who got no credit) and had a Turkish theme. It was known that Emperor Joseph was, at the moment, fascinated with all things Turkish. Of course, not he, nor the librettist, nor Mozart really knew anything about Turkey, except that it was an exotic place and that Turkish noblemen were allowed to have innumerable wives. The opera, much to Mozart's delight, was to be written in German.

He took the theme and made a delightful, funny story with amusing and lovable characters. For the first time he used an idea that would recur often. In the story, the maid who served the heroine was smarter and braver than her mistress and got her mistress out of trouble. The opera was performed under the sponsorship of the emperor and was considered a great success. *The Abduction from the Seraglio* was the first completely German opera. It used some of the style of Italian comic opera. However, the language and the music were more in line with the work of German composers than with those of Italy and France.

Based on the success of his opera, Mozart believed he could support a wife. He married Constanze (whose name he had used for the heroine of his opera) on August 3, 1782, without his father's permission.

Marriage in Real Life and in Opera

Mozart was doing better financially than he had ever done before, but when he had a few extra gulden, he spent them immediately. Constanze seemed to know little about housekeeping, and so their finances were often in a mess.

The Mozarts moved twelve times in their nine years of marriage. Only once did they manage to find adequate quarters, when a rich patron, who loved Mozart's music, went on a long trip and lent them his house. Their happiest time was spent there.

Their most serious problem was a medical one. For six years out of nine, Constanze was either pregnant or recovering from childbirth. Even a young, healthy woman with good medical care would suffer from so many pregnancies. But Constanze was rather delicate, and, of course, medical care was almost nonexistent.

Despite Mozart's problems, the first eight years of marriage were musically his most productive. He was in a circle of excellent musicians who got together several times a week to play for each other and who composed special pieces for those evenings. Some of Mozart's finest chamber music (music that requires just a few players) was created during that time. Much of it was probably heard only by the musicians who were his friends and colleagues. In the best musical circles, he was one of the most admired musicians in Vienna. At court, however, he was ignored. The emperor had decided that his attempt to introduce German music was a failure and had turned back to French and Italian composers. The principal influence at court was an Italian composer called Antonio Salieri. Actually, he was an adequate musician. Many of his pieces are occasionally played today. But he was not a musical genius like Mozart, and he knew it. He was insanely jealous and hostile to Wolfgang (who was quite unsuspicious, and rather liked the Italian), and tried to make sure that he got as little work as possible.

Although Mozart had an enemy at court, he also had a friend. At a masked ball, Mozart met a man named Lorenzo Da Ponte, who would influence his opera career more, perhaps, than anyone else except his father. Da Ponte was the newly appointed court opera-poet.

Mozart and Da Ponte got along famously right from the start. It turned out that they had very similar ideas. Both wanted to write operas that made dramatic sense, with characters that would seem as real as the people they knew.

The two talked of collaborating on a text and a score. But the time was not yet ripe for the new court poet and the man the emperor considered one of Vienna's minor composers to propose that they be commissioned to write an opera together.

That year, Nannerl finally did something that made Mozart's father thoroughly happy. She married into the aristocracy: a genuine baron, Berthold zu Sonnenberg, who was not only titled but rich. What's more, he lived in a castle very near Salzburg. Nobody seemed to mind that the baron was much older than his bride and had several children.

Having one child respectably settled softened Leopold. He started writing to Wolfgang again, and even visited him and Constanze (whom he still criticized constantly) several times.

Mozart continued to write brilliant concertos and symphonies that were performed in his home and in the homes of his various patrons. For the first time he tried to keep his finances in order too. Still everybody in Vienna who knew the Mozarts also knew that even though they generally managed to pay their bills, they never had an extra gulden to their name. Mozart and his wife hoped this would change. They believed that some day Mozart would write his opera with Da Ponte, and they would be rich and famous.

Meanwhile, in France, a very popular writer, Pierre de Beaumarchais, had produced a comedy for the court theater called *The Barber of Seville.* An Italian composer who had also worked at the Vienna court used the play as the text for an opera. Mozart didn't like the music, but he loved the play. Mozart discussed with Da Ponte whether it might be possible to use the Beaumarchais plot for their opera. They discarded this idea when they heard that Beaumarchais had written a sequel called *The Marriage of Figaro.* This play dealt with a barber and valet named Figaro; his bride-to-be, Susannah; Count Almaviva, who was Figaro's employer; and Rosina, the woman whom Almaviva courted in the first play and had married by the time of the second.

Count Almaviva was presented as a tyrannical woman chaser who forced his female servants into unwanted love affairs. Figaro resented the fact that Almaviva was trying to seduce Susannah, and that under law and following custom, there was nothing he could do to protect her. The court was shown as corrupt, and both the judiciary and the church were shown as permitting corruption and injustice to flourish. The play was banned in France where revolution was in the air, and Beaumarchais was suspected of being a secret enemy of the monarchy.

Mozart and Da Ponte read *The Marriage of Figaro* and loved it. Here were real characters who acted like the people they knew, not stick figures who stood around stiffly expressing unoriginal ideas. The clever, loving Figaro despised his master, but had to be careful not to lose his job. Susannah could not afford to object to her woman-chasing master, Almaviva, who hypocritically condemned vice and was unreasonably jealous of the wife he constantly betrayed. And the Countess Rosina was heartbroken at losing her husband's love and respect. All were the kind of people with whom an audience could identify. Here were the makings of the opera Mozart had always dreamed of writing.

For the time being, however, there was little chance that Mozart would get a commission to write an opera from Emperor Joseph or anybody else. The emperor still insisted on Italian operas, and although Mozart occasionally got to write a dance, a sonata, or a quartet for the court, Joseph obviously did not think that he was capable of writing a major work.

The fact that Mozart got any work at all was due partially to Joseph Haydn, one of Austria's most famous composers. Haydn admired Mozart and told anybody who would listen that the much younger man was a genius whose extraordinary talents would be recognized eventually by the music world.

Meanwhile, Mozart's few friends at the court, especially Da Ponte, also praised Mozart at every opportunity. Da Ponte, who wanted to do a production of *The Marriage of Figaro* almost as much as Mozart, used flattery to persuade the emperor that a popular, enlightened ruler would be commended for having this harmless comedy performed at his court.

There was a good deal of rivalry between the German and the Austrian courts. Joseph always considered himself more cultured, more intelligent, more open-minded, and especially more popular with his people than the German rulers, whom he occasionally referred to as "boar hunting barbarians." Da Ponte kept telling Joseph that the Germans did not have the intelligence to understand this subtle, amusing, and very modern play. Joseph could prove his superiority by commissioning him to base an opera libretto on it. Da Ponte also made it clear that he and Mozart were a team. No Mozart, no opera. When several German courts banned the play, Mozart's clever friend succeeded in persuading the emperor to let the opera be written.

The commission finally came through, and the text and music were written, but Mozart's problems were not yet over. The Italian musicians at court did everything they could do to ruin the performance. They persuaded some of the singers to make mistakes deliberately. They also persuaded scene designers and others to slow down their work so that the opera would simply not be ready for its first performance. Da Ponte realized what was happening and went to the emperor to tell him that the musical staff was deliberately trying to ruin the work. Joseph called in the director of the Vienna opera house, the singers, and the orchestra, and told them that if they continued to misbehave, they might all be fired. This was a clear victory for Mozart, perhaps the only one in his life.

The Marriage of Figaro was performed beautifully, with Mozart conducting. In spite of hateful criticism from some of his colleagues, the court and the public loved it. *The Marriage of Figaro* is still considered by many music lovers to be the greatest opera of all time. Unfortunately, it did not bring Mozart either fame or fortune. He was paid his commission fee of 450 gulden (about $250). There were no royalties, no extra money for repeat performances, and no fees for the composer when singers in other parts of Europe sang those lovely arias. That was the way the music world was run in those days.

Last Years

The opera, into which Mozart had poured all his love and talent, was a huge success, but the Mozarts were poorer than ever. Emperor Joseph gave him a nominal appointment at court with a tiny salary, which was much less than the salary that the least talented of the Italian composers were getting.

Mozart, however, had some Irish friends who had received an invitation to go to the British court, known to be much more generous to its musicians than any other court in Europe. *Figaro* had been a great success in Prague as well as in Vienna, and the British court wanted the opera performed in London with the Irish singers who had had leading roles in the Austrian production. The singers were going to England anyway and urged Mozart to accompany them. There, they said, he would be able to make his fortune.

By this time Wolfgang and Constanze had two young children. They would not be able to go along. The apartment that had been offered in London was too small, and besides, Constanze was recovering from a miscarriage and was not strong enough to care for the children on a long trip. So, for the first time in his adult life, Mozart turned to his father for help. Would he be willing to take the two youngsters for a short time so that he and Constanze could get settled in England? As soon as possible they would send for them.

The answer to his modest request shocked him. Leopold turned him down flat and also let him know that, under no circumstances, should he ask his now married sister, Nannerl, to take the boys. We don't know exactly what the rejection letter contained because Constanze burned it, but according to her and to friends, Wolfgang wept for weeks.

The trip to London was off. And the Mozarts were, as usual, broke. An invitation to come to Prague, the city where *Figaro* was without question the hit of the musical season, saved them from having to borrow money as they had many times before. They took the children with them.

In Prague, Mozart was greeted like a major celebrity, something that had never happened to him before. He gave concerts, got commissions for various orchestra pieces (including the Prague Symphony), and was the guest of honor at nightly parties. However, although *Figaro* was playing at the opera several times a week, he did not get another penny for the work. Again, since there were no laws providing royalties for composers, the vast amounts of money made on ticket sales went to the manager of the opera house, Bondini, who had been on the verge of bankruptcy himself before staging *Figaro*.

Mozart did, however, get a commission to write another opera. Since the success of *Figaro* he had discussed doing a work based in part on the life of an aristocrat who was known as an international womanizer and scoundrel. The man's name was Casanova. Da Ponte had met him and was fascinated by him.

While in Prague, Mozart made a brief outline of how such an opera might look and sound. Bondini, with dreams of golden coins dancing in his head (for himself, it not necessarily for Mozart), gave the project his enthusiastic approval and promised to give it its first performance at the height of the next Prague opera season. The opera was to be called *Don Giovanni.*

Back in Vienna Constanze got sick and her doctor sent her off to take the waters at an expensive resort, as he had often done before. This was a usual cure in those days.

With Constanze away Mozart, who was also ill, sat in bed writing the music for *Don Giovanni* by day and dragged himself out to visit cafés and wine bars at night. Miraculously, he was able to finish the work before the deadline. Then he and Constanze somehow managed to get themselves back to Prague by coach, with Mozart making changes and corrections in his score until they actually arrived at the door of their hotel. Da Ponte had written almost all the text until the very last scene, which Mozart apparently completed on his own.

When the ghost of the Commandant, whom the Don has killed in a duel, comes to a dinner to which the Don has invited him, he offers the Don a choice between repenting for his life or dying and going to hell. The Don refuses to make any excuses for the way he has lived. He lets the ghost know that he has always behaved like the person he is and that he would not change his life now even if he could. Was that Mozart talking for the last time to his father? Some Mozart biographers believe that this was indeed the case.

The opera opened in Prague and was an even greater success than *Figaro.* Bondini scheduled it over and over again, and it made him a rich man. Mozart got his one-time composer's fee, plus an additional fee for conducting a performance.

Then Emperor Joseph, who had not been a generous patron but who at least had commissioned some music, died. His brother, crowned Leopold II, cared nothing for music at all. He thought that all he needed was a few military bands.

Soon after the coronation of the new emperor, a strange, unknown man in a black coat came to Mozart's door. Wolfgang was very sick that day, and he was convinced that the man was death, perhaps his father, who was now dead. Mozart was promised a large sum (with a small advance) for composing a requiem (a mass for the dead) for an unknown person. He was convinced that this person was himself and that he would die soon. But he set to work on the mass, and worked on it until the afternoon of his death. It was never finished. As it turned out, the mysterious stranger was no ghostly visitor: He was the servant of a rich and vain aristocrat who wished his friends to believe that he was a great composer. Since he could not write one note of music, he was in the habit of commissioning composers to write for him and then having the works published under his own name. But Mozart did not know this, and whenever he had time he worked on the Requiem.

And now we come at last to *The Magic Flute*. Several years before, Mozart had joined a lodge called the Freemasons. At the time he joined, the lodge was not considered legal, but most members of the court thought it was a harmless group. It preached equality and brotherly love, which did not sound particularly revolutionary to anyone. But the new emperor and his counselors heard that the Freemasons in France were involved in anti-royalist activities. Leaders of the Catholic church also heard that among the symbols used by the lodge were the Egyptian gods Isis and Osiris, which sounded anti-Christian to them. So an order banning the lodge from Austria was issued. Many of the prominent people who had joined in the beginning when the Freemasons sounded like an interesting novelty quit promptly. But Mozart stayed, along with many of the artists and writers in town.

It was at a Freemason meeting that he met an old acquaintance, Emanuel Schickaneder, the theatrical manager. At the moment, he was running a small theater on the outskirts of Vienna called Theater auf der Wieden (theater in the meadow). Most of his customers were working-class families with children, who left the city for a day in the country and visited the theater to see clowns, acrobats, and, occasionally, simple amusing comedies.

From the descriptions available, the programs were similar to early vaudeville. If Mozart produced an opera there, he would be putting himself outside "respectable" musical circles. But Mozart needed work, and the discussions that the two men had had about a fairy tale sort of opera were taken up again. This was the kind of family entertainment that Schickaneder felt might work in his theater. Actually, Mozart had thought off and on for the last ten years about doing a fairy-tale opera. Now he came up with the idea for *The Magic Flute,* combining some of his original thoughts with Masonic lore. He approached Da Ponte with the idea, but Da Ponte said that he could not collaborate this time. He was going to England: There were no chances in Vienna under the new emperor to get the kind of fees he was used to getting. Losing Da Ponte was a serious blow to Mozart. He had never written a libretto and knew of no one whom he wanted to trust with it.

His lodge brothers became interested in the idea and offered their services as writers. So did Schickaneder, who had written a few sketches for his theatrical productions in the past. The first draft of *The Magic Flute* looked exactly like a play written by a committee, which is what it was. We do not really know who wrote the final version, but many of Mozart's biographers believe that Mozart himself had a great deal to do with it. Certainly the characters of Papageno and Papagena are the kind of creatures that Mozart loved. Much of the humor in the opera is also similar to the kind of comedy Mozart liked best, and it is almost certainly different from the earnest morality of the Freemasons and the simple farce of Schickaneder.

Mozart now had two major commissions, the Requiem and *The Magic Flute.* His fame in Europe was spreading, even though in Vienna he was still mainly known for his inability to pay his bills.

KENT STATE UNIVERSITY LIBRARY, KENT, OHIO

When he received a commission from Prague to write another opera, *La Clemenza di Tito,* he traveled there even though he was ill. He did what was asked because he needed the money.

By the time Mozart returned from Prague, he was seriously ill. His health broke down completely in November. His limbs swelled, he could keep neither food nor water down, and he ran a high fever. Often he was in severe pain. He also began to imagine that he was being poisoned by his enemies, in particular Salieri. Various facts tend to make this seem quite impossible. In the first place, Salieri was no longer in Vienna. In the second place, he may have disliked Mozart, but he was not the kind of man to kill anybody. And in the third place, Mozart's symptoms (including his feverish fears and accusations) point to kidney failure, brought on by years of neglect made worse by a sudden, overwhelming infection.

In spite of his illness, he managed to finish *The Magic Flute,* which was performed at Schickaneder's theater in the park. The first performance was the last music Mozart ever conducted. The public loved the opera; the aristocracy took little notice of it. But like his other operas, it became very popular. This fairy tale, by a man whose life had been anything but a fairy tale, was Mozart's final achievement.

December 4, the afternoon of Mozart's death, he was still working on the Requiem. He and a few friends sang some of the sections, while a copyist took down the music, since Mozart's hands were too swollen and he was too weak to write. That evening he died.

Constanze had to borrow money for the funeral, and he was buried on a freezing, snowy night, similar to the one on which he was born. Constanze was too sick and exhausted by grief to attend the funeral. Less than a dozen of his friends followed the inexpensive, wooden casket. The services took place at the Stefanskirche, one of the smaller churches in Vienna, and he was buried in a grave without a marker. No one today is entirely sure where the grave site actually is.

But, contrary to popular legend, he was not unknown and despised at his death, although he was certainly poor. As a matter of fact, both *Figaro* and *Don Giovanni* played in many of the major European opera houses the year of his death. In concert halls, one could hear his symphonies and his concertos. His career was actually on the rise in his last year. Had he lived a few years longer, he might well have become as famous and prosperous as his father had always hoped he would. In Germany, a young musician, Ludwig van Beethoven, heard of Mozart's death with sorrow and disappointment. He had planned to move to Vienna that year to become Mozart's pupil. He considered Mozart to be the greatest composer in the world.

The Mozart family actually prospered after his death. After several years, Constanze married a man of fortune and substance, George Nikolaus Nissen. He took good care of her and her two sons. After Mozart's death, she worked on his first biography, which was not very accurate. She also preserved all his music, something for which we must be eternally grateful.

The older son, Karl, who had no musical ability, became a successful merchant in Salzburg. The second son, Franz, became a moderately successful conductor and pianist. Neither married, and there were no children. Nannerl also never had a child, and so Mozart had no direct descendants. There is only the music, and that will live forever.

The Magic Flute:
The Story

Actually the story of *The Magic Flute* is quite simple, although when one first watches it, it sounds and looks as if someone were trying to tell several stories at the same time. The reason for this is clear. In most of Mozart's best operas there was one writer (Lorenzo Da Ponte) who worked closely with the composer on producing the story line and the actual text (called the libretto). The two men had very similar ideas about what kinds of operas they wanted produced. They both believed that the text and the music had to strengthen and enhance each other, and that the story had to make sense and the characters had to sound and look real.

The operas on which they had worked together included *Don Giovanni* and *The Marriage of Figaro*. By the time Mozart was commissioned by the Freemasons to write *The Magic Flute*, Da Ponte had left Austria permanently for London, and Mozart was too sick to make the long journey there to consult with him. Also, the Freemasons thought they knew exactly what they wanted: a work that would express their philosophy of life and that would be considered serious and profound. They also insisted on having characters that represented good and evil, not people who had human faults as well as nobility.

The story line that was first presented to Mozart by the Freemasons was the kind of text he had never wanted to use. He thought it would bore the audience, since the characters were not varied enough to allow him to compose the many different strains of music that gave his best operas their magic. He felt that the proposed libretto was more preaching than art.

In several of his letters he told his wife and sister how much he missed Da Ponte, who might have been able to turn this rather dreary material into something lively, interesting, and fun. In the end, he may have taken the text home and rewritten some of it, probably persuading the Freemasons to let him include two characters who gave the new opera some of its magic and most amusing moments, as well as a good deal of its best music. These were Papageno and Papagena, half-bird, half-human creatures who in many ways resembled the peasant and servant characters that had added so much to the success of some of his other operas.

So we now have an opera that is (a) a fairy tale, (b) a piece that preaches the ideas of the Freemasons, and (c) a story with some amusing and lighthearted elements that, in the end, were the main reason for its success.

Mozart enjoyed the kind of popular magic and variety shows that were performed not in opera houses but in the amusement parks where Vienna's families often took their children on weekends. He loved what movie directors now call special effects: fire, storms, deep fog, waterfalls, and other events that were very hard to manage on the simple stages of Europe's old opera houses. However, on the outdoor stages of the amusement parks, producers often experimented with fireworks, actors who disappeared down trapdoors and re-appeared magically on another part of the stage, and similar stage tricks. Since *The Magic Flute* had not only been commissioned by the Freemasons, but also by Schickaneder, Mozart had a chance to experiment with the kinds of stagecraft he thought would bring a different audience into the theater. *The Magic Flute* was not just for the aristocracy, but for the plain folks of Vienna for whom opera was too highbrow and expensive. He also thought that with Papageno and Papagena as characters, children might enjoy the new work. He was right. *The Magic Flute* became a huge hit. It not only attracted the usual crowd of weekend park visitors, but even brought the aristocrats out of Vienna. They generally considered these parks vulgar but came to see the new, unusual work.

The Story

As the curtain opens, the audience sees a young man called Tamino wandering around the stage, looking lost and bewildered. He tells us that he does not know what country he is in, that he has no idea how he got there, and that he wishes he could find his way home. As he turns around, he is confronted by a huge, fire-spitting snake that is ready to attack him. Unlike the usual hero, he does not draw his sword to fight and defeat the beast, instead he shakes with horror and faints from pure fright. (This is a typical Mozart touch. Who else would

have his hero react to danger by almost dying of fear?)

As the young man lies on the ground, with the snake ready to eat him alive, three beautiful ladies appear. They make short work of the monster, killing it with a knife and stick. Then they proceed to give the hero first aid, making him drink some water and waving their shawls to give him air. He wakes up and finds the dead monster. He also sees a strange birdman, who turns out to be the bird catcher Papageno, and the helpful ladies who are competing for his attention, and praising his handsome appearance.

He tells them (and the audience) that he is a prince from a foreign land, that he is lost and would like to get home.

The ladies inform him that they are servants of a powerful and generous ruler, the Queen of the Night. They will have to

report his presence to her because he is a stranger in her king-
dom. They leave, talking about Tamino to one another.

Tamino is left with the strange looking individual who is half
man and half bird. Unlike the evil snake, he is not one bit frightening. He is round, jolly, and obviously quite pleased with him-

self. He lies that he is the hero
who killed the monster. Tamino is
suitably grateful and asks the
newcomer who he is.

His name is Papageno, and
he, too, works for the Queen of
the Night, catching colorful song-
birds for her ladies-in-waiting,
who keep them as pets. In return,
he receives very good food
(especially delicious cakes and
pastries) and wine. Except for
the fact that he is sometimes
lonely because he is the only
birdman and cannot find a
female friend like himself, he is
generally happy. He is simply delighted with his alleged bravery,
until the ladies return and find
out he has taken credit for slay-
ing the monster.

They put a lock on his mouth
so that he cannot talk, call him
a boasting liar, and let him
know that instead of cakes

and wine he will be getting stones and water for his supper.

For Tamino they have a gift from the Queen, a picture of a lovely young girl. Tamino takes one look at the picture and immediately falls in love. (In fairy tales heroes frequently fall in love with girls whom they have never met even though this almost never happens in real life.)

As he gazes at the picture, there is a tremendous roar of thunder, a mountain separates, and in a shower of stars the Queen of the Night appears. "Do not fear," she tells Tamino. "I wish you only happiness, but I need your help. I am in deep despair because my only daughter, Pamina, the girl in the picture, was literally torn from my arms when she was still a child, kidnapped by her evil father, Sarastro. He keeps her prisoner, locked up in his castle. If you set her free to come back to me, she will be yours if you want her." Tamino assures the Queen that he certainly does want Pamina and will do anything to return her to her mother. There is another crash of thunder, the mountain opens again, and the Queen disappears.

The three ladies remove the lock from Papageno's mouth and order him to help Tamino free Pamina. To Tamino they give a flute, which they say is magic and will save him from the dangers he will encounter on his journey. Papageno also gets a present, a set of magic bells. At this point, three young boys, who the ladies explain are spirits, appear. They will serve as guides to point Tamino and Papageno toward Sarastro's citadel.

Tamino and Papageno set off on their journey. Tamino is eager and enthusiastic. Papageno thinks the whole journey will involve a lot of dangerous hard work, something for which he has little taste.

Next we finally meet the beautiful Pamina, who is locked up in a castle with thick granite walls and iron gates. She is watched by Sarastro's head servant and a group of slaves. The head servant, Monastatos, sends the slaves on an errand and tries to kiss Pamina, who cries out in fear and horror. At that moment, Papageno peers through the window and, because he can fly, manages to get inside to investigate. He looks at the portrait he has with him and realizes at once that he has found Pamina.

The servant leaves to tell his master Sarastro that a strange creature has invaded his daughter's chamber. Papageno takes the opportunity to let Pamina know that a handsome prince, sent by her mother, will soon join them and will help her to escape. "The prince loves you," he says. "He wants to free you so that you will no longer be unhappy, and you and your mother can be together again."

Tamino, meanwhile, is in another part of the citadel in a garden that is faced by three doors, one marked "The Temple of Reason," another "The Temple of Nature," and the third "The Temple of Wisdom." Tamino tries the first door, but is repulsed with the cry, "Go back!" His attempt to enter the second door has the same result. Then, as he approaches the third door, the one marked "Temple of Wisdom," an old man dressed like a priest comes out and asks him what he wants. "Love and virtue," Tamino replies, "and vengeance against Sarastro."

The old man warns him against making hasty judgments. "Almost nothing here is what it seems," he says, "but be patient, and all will become clear to you in time." Then, as mysteriously as he appeared, he leaves.

Tamino is first confused and then terrified. Is Pamina here? And if she is, is she still alive? The magical voices of the three spirits who sent him on his way assure him that she is alive and waiting for him. At this point a large troop of animals—including lions, elephants, zebras, and other wild beasts, along with goats and sheep—come into the garden. The lion doesn't look too friendly, but Tamino starts to play his magic flute and all the animals begin to dance together. The lion even dances with the sheep. This concert is interrupted when Tamino hears Papageno's magic bells and thinks that perhaps the birdman has found the princess. He rushes off to try to find them both.

Just after he leaves, Papageno and Pamina appear, followed by Monastatos and the slaves who are carrying chains and ropes. Now Papageno plays his instrument, and it works as well as the flute. All the would-be captors stop in their tracks and proceed to dance just as the animals did. Pamina and Papageno think they are safe, but instead they are trapped by Sarastro and his priests. "Now there is no escape," Pamina says despairingly. "He always knows everything." She kneels before her father, confessing that she has tried to escape and

get back to her mother. She also tells him that Monastatos has frightened her with his advances.

Sarastro is understanding, and gently explains that he cannot free her because her mother is not fit to guide her. At this time no one knows that the Queen of the Night is really an evil person.

Monastatos now drags in a new captive, Prince Tamino. The two lovers rush into each other's arms, but Monastatos separates them and reports that they have plotted their escape, a fact already known to Sarastro. Since he also knows of Monastatos's conduct toward his daughter, instead of giving Monastatos a reward, he sentences him to a whipping. Sarastro then announces to Pamina and Tamino that he has known of their love, but before they can be together they will have to prove their courage, patience, and perseverance through a series of trials. If they pass, they will be initiated into a community headed by Sarastro. He reveals that far from being evil, he heads a congregation of followers who believe in love, charity, and brotherhood. He also tells Pamina that he took her away because her mother is cruel and wants to use Pamina to destroy "the brotherhood." Just as the old man at the gate had predicted, nothing in this citadel is what it seems.

While Tamino and Pamina are waiting to hear more about what is expected of them, Sarastro assembles the members of his brotherhood in a courtyard to vote on whether, if he passes the difficult tests, Tamino may be accepted as a member. "He wishes to rid himself of the veil of night and enter our realm of eternal goodness," Sarastro says. "He is a prince, fine, just, brave, and virtuous. Do you deem him worthy?"

The priests vote their approval. Sarastro then tells Tamino that he was destined to marry Pamina, which is another reason she was taken from her mother, who might have sold her into a loveless marriage.

Two of the brothers are assigned to act as guides for Tamino and Papageno, who are now to undergo the necessary trials. As they leave, Sarastro prays that the two lovers will have enough courage and wisdom to safely pass the tests.

By now night has fallen and a storm is raging. The two priests

blindfold Tamino and Papageno and lead them into the court-yard of the temple. The blindfolds are removed and the two are left alone. The storm terrifies Papageno, who complains bitterly that he has been hoodwinked into accompanying Tamino on this dangerous adventure, which just might kill them both. Tamino tells him to act like a man. "I wish I were a girl, then I wouldn't have to be brave all the time," Papageno answers.

The priests return, carrying trumpets and torches to light the way, and ask the two men if they are ready to risk their lives in

the tests. Tamino eagerly agrees. Papageno says he'd rather have some wine and pastries or perhaps find a pretty wife. But, out of loyalty to Tamino, he agrees to go along with what he still considers a silly scheme.

To encourage him, the priests tell him that if he succeeds he will indeed find a young bride, the lovely Papagena, who will fulfill all his fondest dreams. Just before the priests leave, one tells the two young men that the tests have begun. The first test is that they must remain silent. Not a word is to be spoken under any circumstances.

As soon as the priests leave, the Queen of the Night's three ladies-in-waiting appear to warn Tamino and Papageno that they will certainly be killed if they betray the Queen. The fearful Papageno begins to proclaim his innocence and is warned by Tamino that he must keep his mouth shut. Suddenly unseen voices and thunder can be heard. They frighten Papageno even more and drive the three ladies away.

The priests return and compliment Tamino on obeying the rule of silence. They also tell Papageno that, although he has not behaved properly, they will give him a second chance.

In another part of the citadel, Pamina is sleeping. She is approached by Monastatos, who again wishes to steal a kiss. There is a clap of thunder, and the Queen of the Night appears, chasing the servant away. Pamina awakens and is overjoyed to see her mother again after so many years. But her joy turns to shock when the Queen hands her a knife and orders her to kill her father. She would never commit murder under any circumstances, Pamina says, and she certainly would never want to hurt Sarastro. The Queen, crying out for vengeance and disowning her daughter, disappears.

Monastatos, who has overheard the scene, threatens Pamina that he will tell her father she was willing to kill him unless she agrees to be his bride. Pamina says she would prefer death to such a fate. "Then die!" roars Monastatos, pointing to the dagger left by the queen at Pamina's throat. Sarastro arrives to save his daughter just in time. He hugs Pamina to comfort her and banishes Monastatos from the community forever. Pamina begs for mercy for her mother. Sarastro again assures her that he has known all along what the scheme was and that he, like anyone who is worthy of being called a virtuous human being, does not take revenge, even against his worst enemies. Father and daughter leave together, arm in arm.

For Tamino and Papageno the trials continue. The priests have left them outside the temple, telling them to remain silent, and wait for the sound of a horn. Papageno, of course, can't stop himself from chattering, but Tamino ignores him.

Papageno complains, first of thirst and then of boredom. A withered old hag enters with a pitcher of water. She sits down next to Papageno and tells him that, in spite of her appearance, she is only eighteen years old and the girlfriend that the priests promised him. Shocked, Papageno asks her name, but before she can answer, there is another thunderclap and a priest reappears, telling Papageno that this is his last chance, not one more word.

To help Papageno stop talking, three spirits enter, bringing along a table laden with delicious food. While Papageno stuffs himself, Tamino plays his flute. Its magical sound travels to Pamina and draws her to Tamino. Pamina rushes in happily and the two lovers are reunited. But Tamino cannot speak to her. He must keep silent. Pamina does not understand. She

thinks that he has lost interest in her, and leaves, feeling dejected and miserable.

Finally, Tamino hears the horn, which means that he must now be ready for further trials. The priests enter and praise him for his behavior so far, but warn him that the coming trials will be much more severe. Pamina is brought in to say farewell, but Tamino still may not speak to her, much to her distress. They are led away in separate directions.

(Incidentally, forbidding a lover to speak or notice his sweetheart was not an original idea either with Mozart or the committee of writers who produced the original story. It had been used before in many fairy tales.)

Tamino departs with the priests, accidentally leaving Papageno behind. Papageno, more frightened than ever by the dark and deserted place, expresses his regret for having joined this crazy mission in the first place.

He is joined by a priest, who lets him know that he has failed for the last time. He will never have a chance to join the brotherhood with Tamino. Papageno, at this point, could not care less. All he wants is a good glass of wine. Magically, it appears. Of course, Papageno is delighted, but he is still lonely. More than ever he wishes for a pretty young wife.

He plays his magic bells and, to his unpleasant surprise, the old hag hobbles back in. "Here I am," she announces. Papageno certainly is not eager to marry her, but she assures him that if he refuses he will be trapped in this spooky place forever. This seems like an even worse fate, so he swears that he will be true to her.

Her rags and wrinkles suddenly fall away, and she is transformed into a lovely young girl, covered with feathers just as

he is. As he reaches out to embrace her, the priest returns to send her away, because he says Papageno is not yet worthy of an award. Papageno is furious, and swears that he will let the earth swallow him up if he is separated from his newly found sweetheart. Immediately the earth rumbles menacingly, and begins to open. He begs the priest to give him just one more chance and follows him into a cavern.

In a small garden the three spirits secretly watch as Pamina rushes in clutching the dagger her mother left behind. She believes that the Queen of the Night has cursed her because she did not follow her orders and, therefore, she has lost Tamino's love. As she is about to kill herself, the three spirits who have been watching her come out and stop her. They assure her that Tamino does indeed love her and that everything will turn out all right. Pamina's actions may seem excessive, but her grief gives Mozart a chance to write one of his wonderful sad songs for her. (He had complained in a letter to a friend that there really was not much for Pamina to do in the opera and that he therefore felt obliged to give her some especially beautiful music.)

Meanwhile, among the rocky peaks of the mountains surrounding the citadel, with barely enough light to see even one foot ahead, Tamino is ready to attempt his first test. In one of the nearby caves he must pass through a blazing wall of fire. In another he must pass through a huge, wild waterfall.

Tamino approaches the tests fearlessly. He stops only when he hears Pamina calling for him to wait. He is told that he may now break his silence, and the couple embraces and declares their love for each other.

Pamina insists on joining Tamino for the two trials and tells

him to play his flute to protect them on their journey. She promises not to leave his side, for, she says, their love will also protect them. With her hand on his shoulder, both enter the cave of fire and walk calmly and fearlessly through the flames. Then together they pass through the raging waterfall. As they emerge from the cave, they are greeted by the brotherhood. They have passed all the tests.

While Tamino and Pamina are in the cave, Papageno looks everywhere for his vanished Papagena. Discouraged, he decides to hang himself from the nearest tree. Again the three spirits appear in the nick of time and remind him that he only has one life to live. Death is permanent; while there is life there is hope. Then they suggest that he play his magic bells. As he plays, the spirits bring in Papagena. The two bird people agree to marry and have many little Papagenos and Papagenas. Hand in hand, they leave to establish their home.

But the Queen of the Night is still plotting revenge on Sarastro, Tamino, and Pamina. She conspires with her three ladies-in-waiting and Monastatos, who has joined her after being exiled from the citadel. The Queen promises Mona-

statos Pamina's hand in marriage if he will help lead her through the secret passages to the inner court of the citadel where she hopes to find and kill her husband and take charge of his brotherhood.

But again Sarastro knows without being told what they are planning. The plotters hear the sound of rushing waters and the earth rumbles under their feet. Suddenly the earth opens, and in a wall of fire they are swallowed up by the eternal night. They have brought doom on themselves by their hatred and their scheming.

In the garden of the citadel, the sun is shining. Sarastro, presiding at the ceremony attended by the entire brotherhood, welcomes both Tamino and Pamina into the fold. Mozart does not make a point of this, but Pamina is clearly the first woman to have been accepted into the society. She has earned the honor by bravely accompanying Tamino through his trials. Praising the courage of the couple, all those assembled celebrate the power of good over evil and of love and virtue over hatred and violence.

The Salzburg Marionettes

Kinds of Puppets

When I was about seven years old, I went to a party at which somebody's uncle gave what seemed like an exceedingly clever and amusing performance. He vanished behind a white screen with a lamp and told the story of *Little Red Riding-Hood,* illustrating it with pictures he made just by moving his hands around. We all thought his wolf was magnificent. The heroine left something to be desired and so did her grandmother. But the grandmother's cat (seen only from the back) looked very catlike. That was probably the first puppet show I ever saw, and it used the simplest material possible to create its effects: a pair of human hands and a lot of imagination.

I have seen many puppet shows since, from the most simple and improvised to the most complicated and carefully rehearsed. Materials used to make the puppets have ranged from pieces of wood, straw, and several dish towels (put together by my children), to complex characters, with faces created by highly trained sculptors, dressed in clothes, and playing in front of scenery created by great artists. Puppet shows have been put on by groups of children on a rainy afternoon, with improvised figures and a cardboard box as a stage, and by groups of highly trained puppeteers before audiences of knowledgeable adults in major theaters throughout the world.

Puppet shows are probably among the oldest entertainments known to man. We know that there were groups of puppeteers who traveled from town to town as early as 500 B.C. There are pictures of performances in ancient Greece, and some Roman dramatists wrote plays for puppets as well as for live actors. Sometimes puppets were used in religious ceremonies. At other times they were prohibited by priests and/or kings because they were believed to be magical and might be used to perform witchcraft. But even during those times when puppet shows were prohibited, children probably got together to create their own performers and to make up their own plays.

From the earliest figures to today's Muppets, puppets have been part of popular culture all over the world. In the Middle Ages, crowds would gather to watch puppeteers who came to town to show their craft and pass around the hat for pennies at the end of the show. Today millions of children watch the inhabitants of Sesame Street, who teach them to read, count, and be kind to their neighbors. Kermit the Frog and Miss Piggy may be among the most famous characters in the world.

Different cultures created their puppets in different ways, but all employ a few basic techniques to make these figures come to life. It is not possible in a book like this to describe all of these methods, but a few of the ones most frequently used can be described.

Shadow Puppets

A shadow puppet performance is a more complicated variation of the kind of play my friend's uncle gave at that party. The puppets are flat figures cut out of paper or wood. These days they have a control rod attached to the neck, and the rest of the body hangs from that point. They are shown in a dark room against a white semitransparent screen that is lighted from behind. The feet of the puppet rest on the foot of the screen, and the screen is usually tilted forward so that the puppet can lean against it and not fall down. Usually a rod is also attached to each arm so that the figure can be moved in various ways by the unseen puppeteer behind the screen. More complicated shadow puppets may have several additional rods and wires, which allow the puppet to move less stiffly.

Shadow puppets are the most popular variety of puppet in the Far East, where the rod and wire technique has been refined to a point where the puppets can be moved in subtle and imaginative ways. They can even dance. Also, color has been added so that the shadows are no longer just black on white. Some of the greatest shadow puppet artists of the past and present have made figures that are of great artistic value. Some puppets from Thailand, especially those made centuries ago, can cost as much as a painting by a major artist. A shadow puppet I admired in a shop in Tokyo turned out to cost over $100,000. It was more than 500 years old.

Glove Puppets

Glove puppets consist of a hollow sculpted wood or clay head with a mitten-like piece of cloth attached, into which the puppeteer puts his hand. These puppets are worked from below, from a booth that is open at the top in front like a small stage. Usually the puppeteer puts his first finger into the hole in the head of the puppet and his thumb and second finger inside its arms. The body and legs hang loose, but the puppeteer is usually careful to keep the legs on the rim of the stage so that it seems as if the puppets are walking. This kind of puppet originated in the Middle Ages, probably in England, and is still popular in parks all over Europe. Occasionally one can see puppet theaters of this sort at country fairs in the United States.

Most of the European glove puppet companies perform traditional stories. The British Punch-and-Judy show is probably one of the oldest.

KENT STATE UNIVERSITY LIBRARY, KENT, OHIO

Actually, it has a very violent plot, which has been changed in most puppet theaters to suit audiences of children. In the original story, Punch is a truly nasty bully, who beats up all his neighbors, throws his baby out of the window because she won't stop crying, and beats Judy until she is unconscious because she objects to his form of baby-sitting.

Incidentally, some of the Muppets are glove puppets, Kermit the Frog for one. Obviously Big Bird is not—nobody would have a large enough hand to move him around the stage.

Rod Puppets

Rod puppets, like shadow and glove puppets, are usually worked from a booth below the stage where the puppeteer hides. The stage itself is similar to the glove puppet stage. These puppets can be made in much larger sizes than glove puppets. They are seen themselves and are not just shadows on a screen. They are made of molded papier-mâché (small pieces of paper mixed with water, creating a texture like Play-Doh). Some puppet faces are made of sculpted wood. The rods are made of strong wire. A main wire goes up the back; smaller wires, like umbrella ribs, are attached at one end to this main wire and at the other end to an arm, hand, leg, foot, neck, or other part of the puppet one may want to move. The whole skeleton is hidden by the puppet's clothes. The puppeteer moves the puppet by pulling on the wires and by occasionally using his hands as he would in a glove puppet.

One of the most complex and beautiful puppets, basically built in the form of a rod puppet, is used in Japan in a special kind of theatrical entertainment called Bunkaru. In Bunkaru theater, the puppeteers work on a very large stage and are not hidden from the audience. They wear black clothing, and black face masks, and after watching a Bunkaru performance for a while, one suddenly realizes that the presence of those puppeteers has been forgotten. It seems as if the often human-size puppets are moving by themselves. The plays are almost always traditional, going back as far as the sixteenth century. These performances are not meant especially for children, although there are sometimes children in the audience. Most large and middle-sized Japanese towns have Bunkaru theaters, and some Japanese go to see the same story performed over and over again, comparing the merits of one troupe with those of another, just as we go to see the same operas or ballets many times and compare the performances.

Marionettes

The Salzburg puppets are marionettes, the most complex of all puppets to make and manipulate. Basically, they are dolls with strings attached to all the body parts and joints that the puppeteer might want to move. The strings in turn are attached to wooden sticks that are held and moved by the puppeteer, who uses his fingers to pull and relax the strings, giving the puppets motion.

Marionettes are worked from above, which means that their theater is also more complicated than the simple box-like structures used for other kinds of puppets.

Marionette theaters are built with scaffolding and walkways above the stage on which the puppeteers can stand and move. The best marionettes look lifelike and move in very lifelike ways. Although the average marionette may range in size from one to two feet, everything on the stage is sized so that they seem much larger. It is always surprising when, during rehearsals or after the audience has left the theater, one sees an actual full-sized human being walk out on the stage and stand next to a puppet. The illusion the puppet creates may be so complete that the puppet looks like the real person, and the person like some kind of giant from outer space.

The Salzburg Marionettes: Actors on Strings

There is a room on the second floor of a small, exceedingly elegant theater in Salzburg populated by hundreds of small people. As one enters that room, one has the feeling that all those people are paying close attention to the visitor. They seem to be looking straight at him or her. Some look friendly and inviting. Others look suspicious. Still others look downright angry. But they definitely seem to establish contact with any human being who enters their space.

The first time one comes into that room, one gets the feeling that one has stepped, uninvited, into a different world. But for some, that world almost immediately becomes a friendly, accepting place. A few find the presence of all those "little people," who are actually dolls on invisible strings, somewhat spooky. But there is no doubt, whatever one's reaction, that the marionettes, especially when they are all sitting in their proper places, have a completely different effect on one from a doll department in a toy store. The puppets can at times seem human.

One young French puppeteer, after working at the Salzburg Marionette Theater for only a few months, said that she visited this room when she felt lonely and homesick, and talked to the dolls. Another puppeteer said he goes there to sort out any problems he might have. He might even ask one of the older, wiser looking marionettes for advice. Of course, the doll never actually answers his questions, but the man says the process helps him to come to his own solutions.

Marionettes have a long and distinguished history in Salzburg, both as pure entertainment and as high art. Starting probably as early as the fifteenth century, touring players with portable theaters traveled to Austria from France and Spain. They set up their theaters in any town that gave them permission and performed as long as they attracted a paying audience. In spite of their popularity, the authorities were often suspicious of what they called "traveling players." In Salzburg, permission was required from the bishop and was rarely granted. The rules said, "It is forbidden to perform such things, which may in some way belittle religion and respectability. Impropriety must be avoided, and the play must end early enough so that the building can be vacated and locked up by eight o'clock."

In Salzburg, almost no puppeteers received permission to set up their little theaters. When a troupe did manage to sneak in and give its play in a park or on a street corner, the troupe was arrested, and they stayed, for a few days, in a very uncomfortable jail. Even that did not discourage all performers, so stricter punishments were instituted. There is a record of an unfortunate puppeteer, Johann Schmid, who was arrested on November 3, 1753, and sentenced to be whipped thirty strokes in public. The chances are that he, for one, did not perform there again.

Nevertheless, puppet shows became more respectable, largely because the aristocracy decided that they made fine entertainment for parties. Troupes began to perform serious plays, including *Romeo and Juliet*, *Hamlet*, and *Dr. Faustus*. Opera singers from the court theater began to perform with the marionettes. And when a puppet theater was built at the royal court in Vienna, Joseph Haydn wrote a series of little operas for it.

Eventually some puppet masters actually became local celebrities. Among those giving approved performances in Salzburg was Otto Aicher, presumably an ancestor of the Aicher family that founded the Salzburg Marionette Theater. He directed a puppet theater at the university where he taught. It is said that he did many spectacular plays and gained great fame throughout the town.

The popularity of marionette theaters spread this time from the aristocracy to the people. Rules against strolling players, including puppeteers, were reintroduced. Archbishop Hieronymus was particularly opposed to what he considered "vulgar and godless entertainment." But it was too late to suppress what had clearly become a form of serious art. In many towns, puppets were the only kind of theater available, and even serious composers and writers were becoming fascinated with marionettes.

In Munich, a puppet artist, Joseph Leonard Schmid, obtained permission to open a permanent public theater. He teamed up with a well-known writer who specialized in fairy tales and other children's stories, Count Franz von Pocci. Schmid used von Pocci's stories, which apparently were not only delightful and exceedingly well written, but which also managed not to annoy either the church or government officials in Munich.

The main character in many of the Schmid plays was Kasperl, a man who got into all kinds of amusing trouble. He had a large red nose and always wore a big hat. Although he did not look like Charlie Chaplin's little tramp, the first major comic hero of American motion pictures, there are similarities between the two characters. They could make people laugh, and they could sometimes make people cry. Most of all, they were good guys who battled the rich, the powerful, and the greedy, and who, after many defeats, won out in the end.

One day in the audience at the Munich puppet theater there was a teacher from the Technical College in Salzburg. He was a sculptor by the name of Anton Aicher. He wanted to learn the techniques of the Munich

Marionette Theater, because he had hopes of opening a similar theater in his hometown. By then, Joseph Leonard Schmid was in his eighties. He had usually refused to take on pupils or to share his technical secrets with would-be puppeteers. He did not want other marionette theaters to open near Munich and draw some of his audience away. Nevertheless, he offered to teach Anton Aicher how to run a marionette theater.

Aicher learned from Schmid but did not copy what Schmid was doing. Aicher had his own ideas about what a marionette theater should be and what kinds of plays he wanted to perform. He first built a theater for his family, inventing new methods of staging plays and creating new characters for his children. In this way he gained the experience he needed to develop a professional theater. He found ways to make the puppets move more excitingly and more smoothly, and to use the stage in more creative ways. Many of the methods he developed to improve his art are still in use today at the Marionette Theater in Salzburg.

Aicher found the Kasperl figure somewhat crude. So he created a new hero, the Salzburg Kasperl, "whose comedy lay in a delicate and sensitive spirit, together with a melancholy attitude and the natural cunning of an innocent child" (*The Salzburg Marionette Theater* by Gottfried Kraus, Residence Verlag, 1966).

For his first public performance, Aicher chose a very early Mozart opera, written when the composer was only eleven years old, *Bastien and Bastienne*. The performance was a huge success and was repeated many times in a large hall in Salzburg. By the end of the first summer, the marionettes had become an important part of the town's summer season.

Today, the theater has a very sophisticated sound system and uses the best available recordings of the operas its puppets act out. In the beginning, however, live singers were used. They were hidden underneath the stage and through a system of mirrors could watch their puppet counterparts and synchronize their voices with the performance.

The whole Aicher family participated in the theater venture. Since Professor Aicher was not allowed to hold two jobs (teaching and running a theater), he eventually gave up his secure teaching position to devote himself to the marionettes. Rearing a family on the proceeds of even a successful marionette theater must have been difficult, perhaps almost as difficult as becoming a freelance musician like Mozart. It is not surprising that when the youngest Aicher son expressed an interest in not attending a university but instead becoming a full-time puppeteer like his father, the whole family firmly opposed the idea. Young Hermann was sent off to the State Institute of Technology in Vienna to learn a money-making profession.

It was Hermann's older brother, Karl, who helped his father run the theater. When Karl died, Hermann begged to be allowed to return to the theater. Eventually he was allowed to quit his studies in Vienna and take over many of his father's duties. Soon he was in charge of the operation. He expanded both the number and type of performances. In 1925 he married a talented young singer, Friedl, and she, too, became active in his work. She was particularly helpful in improving the music, which was still performed by musicians underneath the stage.

The company became well known, first in Germany and then in the rest of Europe. They toured, carrying all their complicated equipment with them. Although they played to enthusiastic audiences, money was often short. Then World War II came and curtailed the theater's work.

Everyone thought that the end of the war would put the puppets back on their busy schedule. But a new problem arose: The theater in which they had been playing was condemned by the Salzburg building department. The company had to find a new performance space. For several years nothing permanent could be found. The company spent much of its time touring and became visitors in their own town.

But, as the Marionettes received superb reviews from art and music critics in other cities, the local authorities decided that space would have to be found so that they could again have a regular, fairly lengthy season in

Salzburg. A new building was included in a major city rebuilding plan in a well-organized music and theater district. Several years later, in 1968, they had their own space.

A technical development, the invention of tape recording equipment that could reproduce music flawlessly and play it through speakers located all over the theater, allowed the management to produce whole operas without the help of singers below the stage. Today the Salzburg Marionettes have one of the best sound systems in the world. It is almost impossible to tell that the music does not come from the puppets' mouths but is recorded. Even though the faces are the only part of the puppets' bodies that cannot be moved by strings, it seems, with the right kind of lighting and placement, that the dolls are actually singing.

The first major full-length opera that Hermann Aicher produced was *The Magic Flute.* For this production, and for the first time, Aicher sought outside help for his stage and costume design. He hired a young man, Günther Schneider-Siemssen, who was not known for his work with puppets, but had only worked on live stage performances. He had just been asked to design a full-length production at the Salzburg Theater Company. But while he was working on that, he would often spend his spare time watching the work of the puppet theater. He seemed the obvious person to create the scenery for *The Magic Flute.* His design required a new kind of stage. Previously, the puppeteers had stood behind the scenery. Now they were placed on a kind of bridge, built on scaffolding above the stage, so that the setting could have greater depth. He also suggested a revolving stage, which is still in use. Actually, the company is still using his entire design for *The Magic Flute.* This design is illustrated in this book.

The new stage made touring more complicated. It had to be taken down and rebuilt at every theater in the world where the company played. The Salzburg Marionettes now traveled with several furniture vans of stage equipment, a stage manager, electricians, sound experts, and other technical personnel, along with the marionette handlers. The staff members put

up the stage in every theater where the company plays. The usual stage crews who are employed by these theaters simply do not have the experience to build the complex and unique structure.

New technology made it possible for the company to produce other complex operas, including *The Marriage of Figaro* and *Don Giovanni.* As the string mechanism also improved, it became possible to make larger dolls, which could execute more difficult movements. The Salzburg Marionettes now have in their repertory two ballets, taught to the doll handlers by expert choreographers. *The Nutcracker* performed by the puppets is extraordinary. Not only are all the steps perfectly executed, but somehow the puppets that make up the corps manage never to get out of step. Nobody in the back of the room ever has to shout, "Together now, girls," as a real ballet master often does during rehearsals. Also, there are no crooked arms or legs, stumbled jumps, or unpointed toes. Marionettes may be the only technically perfect dancers in the world.

The Marionette Theater occupies a building that once was an elegant ballroom and casino. There is enough room for offices, for workshops to

repair and/or build the puppets, and a complete dressmaking establishment in which the elaborate costumes for the marionettes can be created from the designer's sketches, and even the tiniest tears repaired. Günther Schneider-Siemssen still designs the scenery for new productions and is an accepted member of the Marionettes family. He also designs for full-size singers at many of the world's best-known opera houses, including New York City's Metropolitan Opera House.

Gretl Aicher: The Present and the Future

She is a small, sturdy blonde woman. It's difficult to tell her age. When standing on the bridge working one of her favorite puppets, she can look like a dancer. When sitting in her office working on a script or chatting with a visitor, she can look like a very proper Austrian lady. There is no doubt about her hands, though. They look like those of a professional musician. Her fingers are incredibly flexible, as they must be to manipulate both the wooden holders and the many strings attached to each of the marionettes with which she works. Her face can reflect childlike delight when she looks at one of her beloved puppets (Papageno is clearly her favorite in the whole troupe), or it can reflect deep concern when something in a rehearsal is not going quite right. This is Gretl Aicher, the daughter of Hermann Aicher, the undisputed boss of the Salzburg Marionette Company. Even the smallest detail of every performance is finally decided by her.

George Balanchine, the founder of the New York City Ballet, said, "Ballet is not a democracy." Neither is a major puppet company, nor any other permanent group of artistic performers: an orchestra, an opera company, or a repertory theater. If there is not one person who knows what must be done and who has complete artistic control, the whole group usually falls into disarray. Artists, including great puppeteers, tend to be temperamental. There has to be someone who has the final say. Gretl Aicher is that person at the Salzburg Marionette Theater and every member of the company knows it. So does any visitor who spends time behind the scenes.

Of all her talented crew, she is also, without question, the greatest puppeteer. "I sometimes feel as if through my fingers I become the puppet," she says. Watching the performances, it takes only a little time to realize which puppet she is handling. Somehow that puppet moves differently from all the others. The difference is hard to explain, but the puppet seems more alive and human than the rest of the cast. "I don't know myself how I infuse life into my puppets," she says. "That's why it is so difficult to teach. It seems as if my hands and my fingers are completely free, as if they take on a life of their own, and that life becomes the puppet."

She has been a puppeteer for as long as she can remember, first as her father's assistant, then as he got older, his collaborator, and now, since

Hermann Aicher's death, the director of the company. The puppeteers, many of them young and college educated, come from many different countries to study the Salzburg technique. All have to have many skills. They handle the puppets in performance, but they also know how to build and repair puppet bodies and touch up the paint on their faces and hands. Everybody can use a needle and thread to fix a costume in an emergency. There are lighting specialists and scene changers, but between acts the whole company works together to put up new scenery, to check that all the props are on the stage, and to look over every string on every puppet to make sure that there will be no mechanical problems.

Productions are rehearsed for weeks. New works are rehearsed sometimes for months. It may take longer to put together a new production at the Marionette Theater than at a major opera house. For a new work there are sound rehearsals, lighting rehearsals, and dress rehearsals that are as lengthy and tense as those of any company of live performing artists.

By the time the lights in the glass chandeliers that hang from the ceiling of the lovely little theater flicker to signal the beginning of a performance, everything must be perfect, and as regular members of the audience (there are many) will tell you, everything always is.

Gretl Aicher has no direct or indirect descendants to whom the company can be passed down when she finally has to leave it. The Salzburg Marionettes have always been a family affair, and their future worries her at times. But to someone who has watched them often over the years, it is obvious that the Aicher family has built a firm tradition, which will form the foundation for the company's future. Probably as long as there are puppet companies in the world, the Salzburg Marionettes will be in the forefront. There will be changes, partly as a result of improved technology, and partly as a result of a changed staff. But the puppets will sing and dance, make us laugh and cry, entertain us, and teach us because, unlike real people, they are truly immortal. As a matter of fact, they never even age.

Bibliography

Anderson, E., ed. *The Letters of Mozart and His Family*. London, 1966.

Davenport, Marcia. *Wolfgang Amadeus Mozart, The Man and the Musician*. New York: Avon, 1979.

Fraser, Peter. *Puppets and Puppetry*. London: B. T. Batsford, Ltd., 1980.

Hildesheimer, Wolfgang. *Mozart*. New York: Vintage Books, 1982.

Kraus, Gottfried. *Das Kleine Welttheater*. Otto Müller Verlag, Hugendubel.

Kraus, Gottfried. *The Salzburg Marionette Theater*. Vienna: Residenz Verlag, 1966.

Landon, H. C. Robbins. *1791: Mozart's Last Year*. New York: Schirmer Books, 1988.

Landon, H. C. Robbins. *The Golden Years*. New York: Schirmer Books, 1989.

Landon, H. C. Robbins. *The Complete Mozart Compendium*. New York: Schirmer Books, 1990.

Malkin, Michael R. *Traditional Folk Puppets of the World*. London: B. T. Batsford, Ltd., 1980.

Marshall, Robert E. *Mozart Speaks*. New York: Schirmer Books, 1991.

Osborne, Charles. *The Complete Operas of Mozart*. New York: Atheneum, 1978.

Schikaneder, Emanuel. *The Magic Flute*. Text for the opera. Translated by Ruth and Thomas Martin. New York and London: G. Schirmer, 1941.

Tomb, Eric. *Wolfgang Amadeus Mozart*. Santa Barbara: Bellerophon Books, 1991.